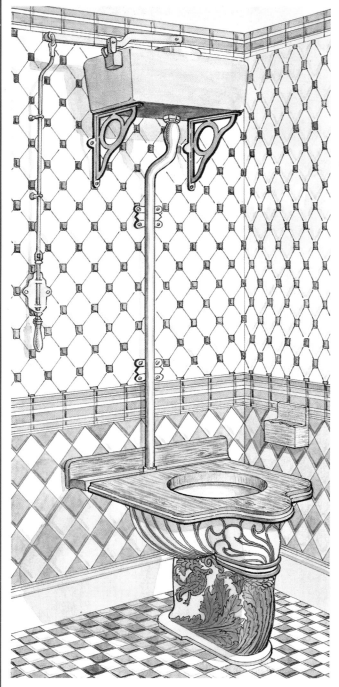

KEEPING
CLEAN

A very peculiar history

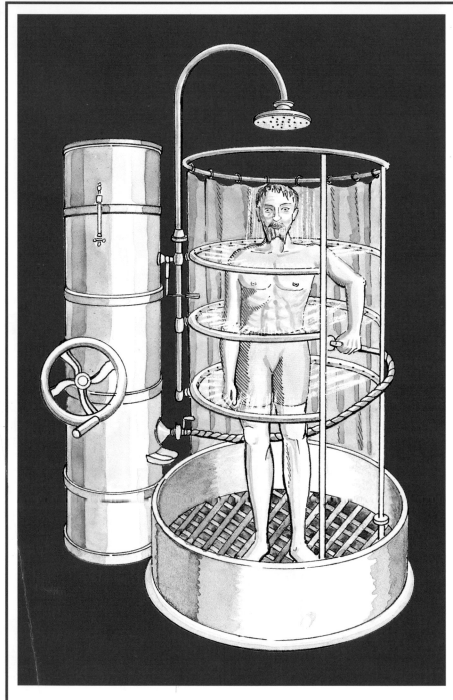

SERIES EDITOR	DAVID SALARIYA
EDITOR	PENNY CLARKE
ASSISTANT	APRIL MCCROSKIE
ARTISTS	DAVID ANTRAM
	SIMON CALDER
	CAROLYN SCRACE
	JOHN JAMES
	JOE MCEWAN
	LEE PETERS
	GERALD WOOD
RESEARCH	RUTH NASON
	MICHAEL NASON

DAVID SALARIYA was born in Dundee, Scotland, where he studied illustration and printmaking. He has illustrated a wide range of books and has created many new series of books for publishers in the UK and overseas. In 1989 he established the Salariya Book Company.

DAISY KERR has written many books on historical topics for both adults and children. She is a part-time adult-education tutor and has contributed to a number of television programmes.

First published in 1995 by Watts Books

Watts Books
96 Leonard Street
London EC2A 4RH

© The Salariya Book Co Ltd MCMXCV

ISBN 0-7496-1613-X

Printed in Belgium

A CIP catalogue record for this book is available from the British Library.

Acknowledgement
The publishers would like to thank Wendage Pollution Control Ltd for permission to reproduce the illustration of the "BioLet®" on page 42.

KEEPING
CLEAN

A very peculiar history

Written by
DAISY KERR

Created and designed by
DAVID SALARIYA

WATTS BOOKS

LONDON NEW YORK SYDNEY

CONTENTS

INTRODUCTION

H ow would you like to bathe naked in Rome, surrounded by 1600 other people? Or to make polite conversation with medieval monks while using a multi-seater lavatory? Perhaps you would prefer an earth-bath, or an electric bath, or to be wrapped in wet sheets? Could you manage to take a shower in zero-gravity space? At different times and in different places, people have had very different ideas about keeping clean.

Some past places – and peoples – might have been cleaner than present-day polluted cities and their sweaty inhabitants. Medieval European nobles enjoyed warm, scented baths in flower-filled pleasure-gardens. Ottoman ladies met friends for a relaxing afternoon at the Turkish baths. Japanese Samurai warriors plunged into steaming, purifying mountain springs; Native American hunters living beside the mighty Mississippi River went bathing every day.

But the past was not always so pleasant: gutters reeked with filth, dung-heaps swarmed with flies, and velvet-covered "close stools" stank in the corners of palace rooms. Kings and queens bathed once every three weeks. Unwashed Mongol invaders were so thickly infested with lice that they seemed to be covered in fur. Early Christian hermits considered their bodies sinful – so they refused to wash or change their clothes. In this book, you can find out more about the very peculiar history of keeping clean.

THE ANCIENT WORLD: PLANNING AND PLUMBING

Simple technology gives cleanness for all.

Brick lavatory connected to an underground drain at the city of Mohenjo-Daro (in present-day Pakistan) c.2500 B.C.

This vaulted sewer, 2 metres high, carried dirty water away from the great public baths (below) at Mohenjo-Daro.

THE EARLIEST western civilizations developed in areas where three "farming essentials" – fertile soils, mild climates and reliable water supplies – could be found. Farmers growing crops or raising animals in Mesopotamia, Egypt, Greece and the Indus Valley all knew that good water management was essential to protect their fields from floods, droughts or sudden deluges. Farm technology – cisterns, channels and drains – was soon copied to provide fresh water and waste disposal for houses and homes.

Elaborate plumbing was a luxury. Not everyone could afford the brightly-painted bathrooms installed about 1800 B.C. at King Minos's palace in Crete. And only a strong, centralized government could plan the complicated network of pipes and sewers that run for many kilometres underground at Mohenjo-Daro (Pakistan). However, throughout the ancient world, everyone believed that it was good to keep clean.

Cleanliness, symbolizing spiritual purity, became part of religion. Egyptian priests washed four times a day; worshippers bathed in huge ritual pools at Mohenjo-Daro. Sculptors portrayed the Greek gods as "perfect" human figures – healthy, strong and clean.

Terracotta drainpipes from Knossos, Crete, c.2000 B.C. Each section was tapered, to fit snugly together and to produce a varying flow of water. This stopped the drain silting up. The joints were sealed with cement.

Lavatory at Knossos, c.1800 B.C. It had a wooden seat above a baked clay bowl, connected to an underground drain. Water for flushing was kept in a jar nearby.

The queen's bathroom in the royal palace at Knossos, Crete, c.1800 B.C. The bath is made of brightly-painted terracotta.

Prosperous houses were built with shower rooms; poor families took the trouble to carry heavy jars of water home for washing, and dug outdoor pits for lavatory waste.

Lavatory seat made of limestone, from the city of Tel-el-Amarna, Egypt, c.1350 B.C.

Comb, tweezers and cosmetic palette, used by Ancient Egyptian noblewomen.

Wooden lavatory with removable waste jar, from a wealthy Ancient Egyptian home.

(Left) Greek athletes used olive oil to rinse away dirt and sweat. They scraped off surplus oil with a strigil, a curved metal tool.

MOST EGYPTIANS bathed once a day in the River Nile, but rich peoples' homes had shower rooms, too. They contained a shallow stone tray linked to an underground waste-storage jar. Showers were simple; you stood in the stone tray, while servants poured water over you.

strigil

WHERE THERE was no running water, women took baths using large basins of water and sponges. (Below) GREEK WOMEN taking a shower, around 550 B.C. Architects channelled swift-flowing streams through pipes on house roofs to provide constant running water.

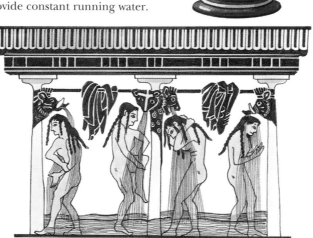

Clay bath tub with a built-in underwater seat from Mycenae, Greece, c.1000 B.C.

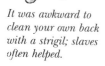

It was awkward to clean your own back with a strigil; slaves often helped.

ROME: PUBLIC CONVENIENCES

Crowded city streets and communal facilities.

Double-seater street lavatory in the Roman colonial city of Timgad, Algeria, c.A.D. 160. The seat and arm-rests are stone.

The city of Rome grew from a few ramshackle huts, built around 800 B.C., to become one of the largest population centres on earth, housing a million people by the 1st century A.D. Like all cities, past and present, it faced problems of housing, transport, food stocks, fresh water and waste disposal. A massive programme of public works was needed to stop citizens dying from epidemics, or being buried under their own filth.

The city's governors planned two major sanitation strategies: aqueducts to bring clean water, and sewers to carry away waste. These were kept running, with repairs and enlargements where necessary, for over 500 years. For sewers, Roman engineers rebuilt underground drains dug by the earlier Etruscan inhabitants in the 6th century B.C. They constructed 425 kilometres of aqueducts, which could carry 350,000,000 litres of water to Rome every day. These were massive projects; one, the Claudian aqueduct, took 14 years to build (with slave labour) and used 500,000 cartloads of stone. The city government was also concerned to safeguard public health. Communal lavatories and local rubbish tips (emptied by slaves) were provided, and 1352 drinking fountains were built.

FRESH WATER from hillside springs was carried to the city of Rome by huge aqueducts. Water flowed along a covered channel supported on tiers of arches. It was used mainly for drinking, but also filled public baths and carried waste away from public lavatories.

Roman insulae (blocks of flats) had communal public lavatories at ground-floor level. They drained into a nearby underground sewer.

drains

PUBLIC BUILDINGS, army camps and even restaurants had communal lavatories. Seats were arranged side by side above a trough filled with running water. There was no toilet paper – sponges on sticks were provided, instead. They were rinsed clean after use. In towns, lavatories were built on street corners. They were smelly and full of flies, especially in summer. Even so, they were more pleasant and hygienic than the alternative: jars of waste in every crowded room.

The Cloaca Maxima – ancient Roman sewers – were extended by Emperor Agrippa (63-12 B.C.). The tunnels were so big (7 metres wide in places) that he could inspect the work by boat.

jar for collecting urine

sponge-stick

stepping stones

Streets in Roman towns were noisy, smelly and very dirty. There was often water running down the road – overflowing from public lavatories or drinking fountains, or thrown there by people in houses or shops nearby. Careful pedestrians used stepping stones, to keep their feet dry.

ROME: SANE MINDS, HEALTHY BODIES

Bathhouses and bathing for rest and relaxation.

"THE GREATEST BLESSING we can ask," wrote the Roman poet, Juvenal (A.D. 58 – 138), "is a sane mind in a healthy body." For many Romans, relaxing and keeping clean by taking regular baths was one of the best ways to achieve this. (Others preferred to escape from dirty, stressful Rome to the peace and quiet of the country.)

Most Roman homes did not have a bathroom. So, for cleanness and relaxation, citizens went with their friends to a bathhouse: a building with several rooms of varying degrees of heat, some dry, some steamy and some with pools. By law, men and women bathed separately – but this rule was sometimes ignored.

There were two different kinds of bathhouse. The majority were small, private establishments, rather like a modern health club, open to members only. Some were exclusive; others were cheaper. Altogether, there were almost a thousand of them by the 3rd century A.D. Rome also had eleven public baths – enormous "fitness centres", like the Baths of Caracalla, catering for up to 1600 bathers at a time. They were given to the city by wealthy statesmen, often as a memorial to themselves.

(Below) The Baths of Caracalla, completed in A.D. 235, were the grandest public baths ever built in Rome. They measured well over a kilometre around the outside walls and covered 11 hectares.

AT THE BATHS

Take off your clothes – you bathe naked. Leave clothes in the apodyterium (changing room).

First, some fitness training – choose athletics, wrestling, fencing, boxing, or ball games.

Start your bath in the sudatorium (hot dry "sweat room") or the caldarium (hot steam room with pool).

Scrape your skin with a strigil to remove sweat and dirt. Swim in the tepidarium (warm pool) to rinse.

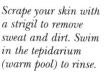

Now, be brave. Plunge into the frigidium (cold pool). It is bracing and will refresh you.

The largest Roman public baths housed shops and offices in rooms built into the tall outside walls.

As well as bathing facilities, Caracalla's baths contained a library and a museum. Citizens could also admire the many fine statues displayed in the extensive courtyards and gardens.

Caracalla's baths contained several vast bathing halls, ranging from the oven-like sudatorium and the tropical caldarium to the gently-warm tepidarium and the open-air frigidarium.

Bathing halls and pools were heated by wood-burning furnaces, sending hot air through underfloor channels. Extra steam for the caldarium came from a giant bronze basin with a fire beneath.

There were also many smaller rooms, some containing little pools or fountains, where individuals could bathe privately or enjoy massage and beauty treatments.

Outside the bathing halls, there were sports tracks, gymnasiums and meeting halls. There were also gardens for sitting or strolling in hot Roman summers.

Roman beauty aids (clockwise from top): Scent bottle, tweezers, ointment spoon, metal mirror, ointment jar.

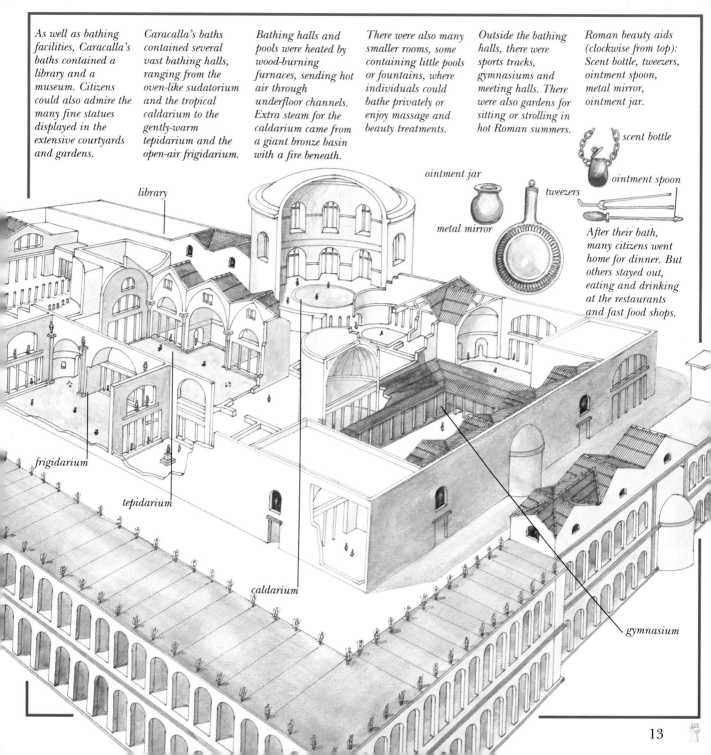

scent bottle

ointment jar

tweezers

ointment spoon

metal mirror

After their bath, many citizens went home for dinner. But others stayed out, eating and drinking at the restaurants and fast food shops.

library

frigidarium

tepidarium

caldarium

gymnasium

CLEANLINESS AND GODLINESS

Religion and the importance of cleanliness.

Pour water from fingertips to wrists.

(Above) Rub hands. (Below) Rinse from wrists to fingertips.

JOHN WESLEY, the 18th-century evangelist who founded the Methodist branch of the Christian faith, used to teach that "cleanliness is next to godliness". Even in Wesley's time, this was a very ancient idea. All over the world, from the earliest recorded history, ritual bathing has been linked to spiritual purification and religious power.

In religious terms, cleansing the body is believed to serve many purposes. It drives out harmful spirits, which may be causing madness or disease. It removes ritual pollution, caused by (for example) touching a dead person. It prepares worshippers for taking part in ceremonies, and permits them to enter a temple or other holy place. It energizes prophets, kings or warriors preparing for a great ordeal. And it marks the change from one stage in life to another, especially from childhood to adulthood.

Ritual bathing need not always involve water. In desert lands, sand or ashes may be sprinkled instead. Fasting or drugs may also be used to "empty" and purify the body, so that anything evil is driven out, and good influences may enter.

MUSLIMS WASH before saying prayers at home or at the mosque. This ritual washing is called "wudu".

Pharisees and Sadducees were two influential groups in Jewish society during the 1st century B.C. They taught that careful observance of traditional Jewish customs, such as ritual handwashing before meals (above), was an essential part of a holy lifestyle.

Like many other Native American nations, the Navaho people, who lived in south-western America, used steam baths to try to cure a wide range of diseases. They believed that steamy heat trapped inside a hogan (hut made of branches) would drive illness away.

THESE STEAM BATHS were combined with purges (drugs to make people vomit, to "cleanse" the body). They were accompanied by prayers and chanting from a shaman – a man or woman who could communicate with the spirit world.

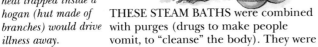

LIKE MANY other religions, the Zoroastrian faith of ancient Persia (Iran) had rituals to purify people who wished to become priests. Candidates were sprinkled with dust, water and urine from a bull (a sacred animal), as they moved through a holy pattern marked on the ground. This "washed" the Corpse Demoness from their bodies. A dog was also present: its pure, keen sight could drive away evil things.

IN JAPAN and Korea, bathers sought spiritual peace and purity by bathing in remote mountain streams. In Japan, there were "magic" volcanic hot springs, too.

The River Ganges in India is sacred to people who follow the Hindu faith. Its life-giving waters nourish their land. There are holy sites where bathers gather at many places along its course. One of the most popular is at Sonepur. In autumn, many hundreds of thousands of pilgrims arrive to take a ritual bath there at the time of the full moon.

MIDDLE AGES: CASTLES AND TOWNS

Dung diggers and the disposal of dirt.

Arrangement of a multi-storey lavatory block, Langley Castle, England. The waste was carried away by a diverted stream.

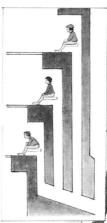

Sanitation was important in medieval castles. Sewage could not be allowed to accumulate inside castle walls, for fear of spreading disease. The solution was to build lavatories (garderobes) that discharged into castle moats, and to stock the moats with fish that fed on the human waste.

YOUR TOWN (or castle) is besieged. Food is running out, and you are exhausted after weeks of fighting. You have faced snipers and cannon balls, and have driven away spies found crawling up garderobe pipes. But now your courage falters. Enemy soldiers are hurling rotting corpses over the walls and floating them in the river (or moat) to pollute your water supply. You are already surrounded by heaps of stinking lavatory waste, and cannot get out to spread this safely on the fields. You fear that dirt and disease will kill you, where bows and arrows have failed.

In the Middle Ages, keeping clean could be a matter of life and death. Castle builders tried to ensure pure water for inhabitants (the best came from deep wells), and plenty of garderobes. Town councils passed laws forbidding the dumping of sewage in streets, and organized refuse collections. They also tried, often unsuccessfully, to keep streams and rivers clean. Even in peace-time, people did their washing, watered their animals and tipped manufacturing waste there. Cloth-making, leather-working and slaughterhouses were especially polluting.

(Right) Communal lavatory at the Archbishop's Palace, Southwell, England, c.1360. (Far right) Plan of the Southwell lavatory.

Plan of garderobe in Tower of London:
1 Outer wall
2 Door
3 Stairs
4 Lavatory
5 Dining Hall

MEDIEVAL TOWNS were built without drains, lavatories or clean water supplies. Rubbish and manure were thrown into the streets.

TOWARDS THE END of the Middle Ages, separate lavatory blocks began to be built, in the hope of making castles cleaner, nicer-smelling places to live.

In 1281 it took 13 men almost a week to remove 20 tonnes of sludge from Newgate Prison lavatory pit, London.

Lavatory above a refuse heap, c.1450. Local councils organized weekly collections of waste. It was spread on fields as fertilizer.

At castles without moats, underground pits were dug to contain waste. In 1183, the floor of the Great Hall at Erfurt Castle, Germany, collapsed. Emperor Frederick and his knights fell 12 metres into the cesspit below. Many drowned.

In houses without lavatories, chamber-pots were used at night. In the morning, they were emptied into the street.

MIDDLE AGES: MANNERS MAKYTH THE MAN?

Washing rituals among members of high society.

ORDINARY MEDIEVAL PEOPLE – servants and traders in towns, and peasants in the countryside – were famous for their lack of manners. They were rough, tough, outspoken and quarrelsome. They would spit in the street, get drunk, be sick and fall into ditches. They had lice, fleas and worms. They had few opportunities to take a bath – their homes had no running water. In summer, men and boys could go swimming in rivers, but for women this was shameful. In spite of these difficulties, some ordinary people prided themselves on being clean.

Things were different for the upper ranks of medieval society. They could afford baths – at home or in the local bathhouse. Cleanliness, plus polite, considerate behaviour, was a sign of good breeding. As William Wykeham, a 14th-century scholar, taught his pupils, "Manners makyth the man". Some young boys had a lot to learn. Books on good manners, written for noble households, found it necessary to warn readers not to blow their nose on the tablecloth, or pick their teeth with a knife.

Pages brought clean water and a clean linen towel so guests could wash their hands before eating and between courses. It was an honour to be invited to wash first. It was also good manners to wipe your lips on a napkin before you drank from the wine goblet.

Water for washing was carried in fancy jugs called ewers. Some had legs, or were shaped like wild men or animals. They might be made of bronze, precious metals, or even decorated with jewels.

An elaborately-decorated laver, or wash-basin, built into the stone wall of a noble's dining-room at Battle Hall, Sussex, c.1330. There was a cistern to store water behind.

PEOPLE WHO could afford it took baths at home. Only the well-off owned a bath-tub and could pay for fuel to heat the water and warm the room. They could pay servants, too, to carry the water (it was very heavy) and to tidy up afterwards.

There were public baths in many towns, where customers could bathe in cloth-lined wooden tubs (to guard against the splinters).

Medieval people got drinking water from wells and streams. It could be carried long-distance in barrels or animal skins.

If you were a brave soldier, or a well-trained young man from a noble family, the king might reward you by making you a knight. But you had to have a bath first. Why was this? Partly, a ritual bath showed you were honest and honourable: it "washed away" all that was bad in your character. It also marked the end of your old status, and the beginning of your new rank in life.

BECOMING A KNIGHT

First of all, take off all your weapons and armour. Carry them to the chapel, to dedicate them to God.

Now, two squires will lead you to the ritual bath. You will be washed, shaved and have your hair cut.

The bathroom is splendid but the bath water is cold. Two old knights lecture you on your duties.

Dressed in a monk's robe, you pray all night in chapel. Next day, the king "dubs" you a knight.

MIDDLE AGES: RELIGION AND RUNNING WATER

Good drainage helps monks to lead a pure life.

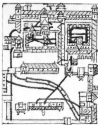

By the 12th century, monks at Canterbury Cathedral, England, had constructed this impressive system of drains and fresh water supplies.

In contrast, peasants living on monastic estates still had to fetch water for drinking and washing from rivers and streams.

NOT JUST ANYONE could become a medieval monk or a nun. To enter the most prestigious monasteries or convents, you had to come from a wealthy and well-connected family. It helped if you had a genuine interest in learning, as well. For many talented men and women, the Church was a high-powered career.

It is perhaps not surprising, therefore, that the buildings housing medieval religious communities were very thoughtfully designed. As children, at home with their prosperous families, monks and nuns had been used to the "best" medieval standards of comfort and cleanliness. Naturally, they wanted to equal or even surpass these in their adult homes. In monastic libraries, they could read about the achievements of Greek and Roman engineers; they used this information to improve their sanitation schemes. On the whole, Church authorities encouraged cleanliness. But they believed spiritual purity was even better. This might be achieved in many different ways, such as fasting, all-night prayers or wearing hair-shirts. Unlike warm baths and hygienic lavatories, they were designed to punish, not pamper, the body.

Monks were expected to wash face, hands and feet before entering church. Nice hot baths were an extra luxury – some monks said they were sinful.

One of the first steps in becoming a monk was receiving the tonsure (a short haircut with a bald patch in the middle) from a bishop.

(Left) Pipes carrying fresh water were made of lead. In wealthy monasteries, plumbers fitted a range of ornamental water-taps.

(Right) Monks were shaved regularly – every three weeks. Barbers used sharp metal razors, and big metal shears to cut hair.

POTTERY URINAL, used by monks. Stale urine collected in such urinals was stored in huge vats at monasteries and other buildings where large numbers of people lived. It was sold to cloth-makers and leather-workers, who used the ammonia in it to help produce high quality goods. Strong solutions of ammonia could remove grease and soften natural fibres. Ammonia also reacted chemically with herbs and minerals to give long-lasting dyes.

urinal

A FEW waste pits from monasteries still survive. By studying the microscopic remains, archaeologists can find out about medieval foods – and medieval illnesses. Some monks had worms; others ate buckthorn seeds as laxatives.

Lay-brothers or monastery servants cleaned out the lavatories – one of the worst jobs in the medieval world.

Over 100 people might live in a large monastery. Plenty of lavatories were needed, like this multi-storey block at Fountains Abbey, Yorkshire.

PORTABLE POTS: COMFORT AND CONVENIENCE

Pots of infinite variety — urinals, chamber-pots and bedpans.

These 5th-century B.C. vase-paintings, (above, and re-drawn, right) show Greek children using potties made of earthenware (baked clay). Potties had holes for legs and a high back to stop the smallest children falling out.

Roman pot – called a "friend" – designed to be hung from a nail on the wall at a convenient height for men to use.

WHAT DO YOU DO when you need to go to the lavatory, but the building you are in does not have one? This problem has faced most people for most of the past. The Romans built public lavatories, and monks, castle-owners and wealthy town-dwellers installed garderobes in walls and towers. But these were exceptional. Most people made use of an earth pit in the backyard, or found a corner in a quiet backstreet. In the countryside, hedges and ditches provided a convenient spot for everyone.

But what happened at night, or if it was pouring with rain, or if you were old, drunk, pregnant, disabled or ill? What about small children? No-one wanted them to make a smelly mess on the floor. What about formal visits to friends? Trips to the theatre? Or sitting in a cold, draughty church? The answer was a bucket, or a portable pot – known as a potty, urinal, chamber-pot, bedpan, jordan, jerry or "bedroom utensil". A shallow, sloping pot, for ladies to use in public under their skirts, was called a "Bordaloue" after a French preacher, famous for his three-hour sermons.

Long-handled earthenware bedpan for invalids, made in the 17th century.

Medieval potters experimented with many different urinal designs.

By around 1500, chamber-pots were made to a standard shape. It stayed the same for centuries.

Medieval pottery – used for drinking-cups and urinals – had to be tough.

19th-century urinal with flared opening, for women's use. Spillage was less likely from bottle-shaped pots like these.

Only the rich could afford chamber-pots. This 17th-century pot, was for a fashionable woman's bedroom.

18th-century women carried small, lightweight pots hidden under their long skirts, to use when out.

Bottle-shaped urinal for men. It has a flat base and was designed to stand on a bedside table.

Fancy chamber-pots might be decorated with "joke" pictures such as an eye or a frog looking up at the user.

New "shovel" design for a bedpan, introduced in the 19th century. It is made of white glazed earthenware which was easy to clean.

"Silent" chamber-pot designed in 1907 in New Zealand. Its maker claimed that the curved inner surface reduced splashing noises.

16th Century: The Sweet Smell of Success?

Queen Elizabeth I and the Ajax flushing lavatory.

IT IS OFTEN difficult to discover what people living in the past really felt. Did they care about smelly close stools standing where everyone could see them? Did they wish there was a better way of disposing of waste than carrying a brimming bucket through the house every morning – or emptying a pot from the bedroom window over the heads of passers-by?

Judging from 16th-century evidence, most ordinary people probably did not mind. But a select few at the court of Queen Elizabeth I of England, including the Queen herself, most certainly did. She prided herself on her extra-sensitive sense of smell – it showed she was "special", and added to her royal mystique. She enjoyed scented creams and perfumes, and always carried a pomander. It covered up any nasty smells that wafted her way, and was meant to protect her from disease, as well.

Sir John Harington, one of Elizabeth's courtiers, won her approval with his successful invention: the first-ever free-standing flushable lavatory. It proved that you no longer needed a stream nearby to have a clean, sweet-smelling convenience. Queen Elizabeth tried it, and was reported to be "well-pleased".

Queen Elizabeth I (ruled 1558-1603) took great care over her appearance: 1 Hair washed with lye (wood ash and water). 2 Skin washed in lotion made from herbs, spices, wine. 3 Teeth cleaned with cloth and toothpick. Scented mouthwash. 4 Herb-scented gloves, stockings, handkerchief.

Gilt and porcelain pomander. Each section contained a different smell, designed to ward off diseases.

Pedlars travelled the country, selling home-made lotions, balms and herbal remedies.

If your fireplace was big enough, you could tip the contents of your chamber-pot into the flames each morning. Men often urinated there, as well. This was smelly, but hygienic. If the fire was burning briskly, its heat killed any germs. But you did run the risk of extinguishing it.

Farmhouses and rich townhouses had "necessaries": back-yard sheds with a wooden seat placed over a bucket of earth. A 16th-century joke told how one man started to say his prayers while sitting in the "necessary". The devil appeared and told him off for speaking holy words in an unclean place.

Courtier Sir John Harington (1560-1612), inventor of the flush lavatory, first built 1594.

*(Right and below) Two of Harington's diagrams of his invention:
1 Surveying the site.
2 The flush system in action. Harington called his invention the "Ajax", a pun on "jakes", the slang word for lavatory.*

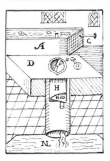

ROYALTY AND RICH people had close stools (chamber-pots concealed beneath padded seats) in many rooms. They were luxurious, but difficult to clean. This 16th-century close stool from Hampton Court Palace near London is covered with cushioned velvet.

Harington's "Ajax" worked by raising a lever to open the drain-cover at the bottom of the lavatory pan. This released a flush of water from the cistern above.

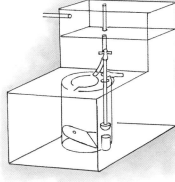

17TH CENTURY: ROYAL SPLENDOUR, ROYAL STINK

Splendour and squalour in the century's greatest palace.

King Charles II of England (1660-1685), famous for rarely washing.

King Louis XIV of France. Every day his face was washed with spirits of wine.

WEALTH MAKES it easier to keep clean, but great riches and great cleanliness did not always go hand in hand. In the 17th century, the poorest inhabitants of Middle Eastern towns could enjoy a trip to the publicly-funded steam baths. Poor Scandinavian farmers needed only a few hot stones, a rough wooden hut and a nearby lake to enjoy a health-giving sauna.

By contrast, King Louis XVI of France (1638-1715), one of the richest men in the world, was surrounded by squalor. He lived elegantly in a magnificent palace, designed to reflect his power and glory. But, to the disgust of certain Parisian visitors, after a number of years this splendid palace began to give off a pungent "lavatory" smell all of its own. No one had considered the sanitary needs of the thousands of courtiers, servants, messengers (and their horses) who came to the palace each day, seeking royal gifts and favours.

Water was pumped from these works at Marly (about 15km) to supply the great fountains at Versailles.

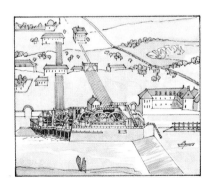

Beautiful fountains were a fashionable feature in rich cities and royal gardens.

IN VENICE, Italy, fashionable women wore high platform shoes, known as chopines. They were based on traditional clogs, originally designed to raise the wearer's feet above mud and sewage in the streets.

chopines

Close stools were often disguised – here, as a stack of 17th-century French books. But their smell often gave them away. As a joke, these books are titled 'Journey to the Nether (that is bottom) Lands.'

close stool

funnel

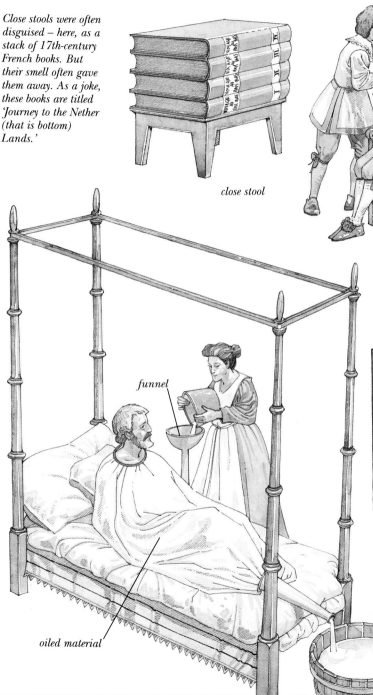

oiled material

Kings, nobles and courtiers all spent time on their appearance. Hair and beards were washed, trimmed and scented; hands and faces were washed, then softened with creams. Teeth were cleaned by chewing twigs or liquorice roots, and polished with salt or powdered chalk.

Elegant outdoor amusements, like picnics and bathing parties, were popular among rich young people. Paintings showing semi-naked bathers were also admired.

HOUSEWIVES were expected to nurse their relatives, often using medicines from secret family recipes. Invalids and old people could be bathed in bed, using a "tent" of closely-woven oiled material, which was reasonably waterproof. A tub collected the "bathwater" at the foot of the bed. Doctors did not agree on whether bathing was healthy or not. Some said it was weakening. It must have been chilly, except in very well-heated rooms.

18TH CENTURY: ELEGANCE AND NECESSITY

Elegance on shore, back to basics at sea.

Mechanical pumps, which raised water from natural springs underground, were the only source of water in many towns.

WEALTHY FAMILIES had servants to carry water from street pumps, so they could wash privately in bedrooms, using furniture like this washstand.

SKILLED CABINET-MAKERS were employed by noble families to design furniture, like this combined wash basin, bidet and chamber-pot.

S OMETIMES, THE 18th century is called "the summit of European civilization". That is a very vague description, but many people would agree that some of Europe's finest country houses, most beautiful cities, most graceful furniture, exquisite clothes and inspiring music were produced then.

All this was only for the rich, of course; poor people still lived in crowded, dirty conditions. But for the leaders of society, elegant neatness was in fashion. Although regular bathing was still a novelty, they wanted their new homes to be airy, clean and refined. They commissioned top designers to make baths and washing cabinets in the latest furniture styles.

Scientific study was also fashionable. A few gentlemen inventors – as well as traditional craftsmen – experimented with plumbing and lavatory designs. Watchmaker Alexander Cumming invented a "stink–trap" to stop sewage smells rising into rooms in 1775. Cabinet-maker Joseph Bramah made an improved flushing lavatory. These developments were closely studied by naval engineers.

Warships and merchant ships now regularly made very long voyages. Could sanitation at sea be improved?

Owners of stately homes liked to install the most up-to-date features, like this plunge bath at Wimpole Hall, Cambridgeshire.

In wealthy Parisian homes, baths were designed to look like fashionable salon furniture.

On board ship it was important to keep clean. Otherwise, disease could quickly kill all on board during a long voyage.

The upper deck of ships was washed daily with sea water, which was a mild disinfectant because of the salt it contained.

heads

pissdales

Lavatories for the crew were known as the "heads", because they were at the bow (front or head) of the ship. They overhung the water, so waste would fall straight into the sea.

Officers and privileged passengers had private lavatories – buckets with seats – in their cabins. Below decks, there was also a communal lavatory for petty officers known as the "roundhouse".

round house

FOR EMERGENCY use on Royal Navy warships, "pissdales" (lead or copper basins with spouts to carry waste overboard) were installed on gun-decks, close to the cannon. They were used by all ranks.

Inventors built experimental lavatories for use on ships and shore. In 1778, Joseph Bramah designed a valve which produced a powerful flush of water; he added the new stink-trap to his lavatory, too.

Bathers in the naturally-hot springs at the Cross Bath, in Bath, 1738.

WATER IS GOOD FOR YOU

"Taking the waters" and sea-bathing are fashionable.

DURING THE MEDIEVAL CENTURIES, many European doctors warned that immersing your body in water was dangerous. Church leaders and town councils also disapproved of bathing; they said – with some truth – that public bathhouses were used as brothels, and were therefore "haunts of sin".

Towards the end of the Middle Ages, medical attitudes changed. In 1326, sick people who drank the waters of a bubbling spring at Espa, in present-day Belgium, claimed that it cured their diseases. Many people believed them, and a new fashion developed for "taking the waters", that is, drinking them and bathing in them. Espa became the first "Spa" resort town, making a living from its healthy water supply. It was soon copied by rival towns, such as Bath in England, Baden-Baden in Germany, Vichy in France and Arrowhead in America. Places with natural hot or bubbling springs in many other countries, from Iceland to Japan, also became popular tourist resorts.

English eccentric Dr Graham ordered his patients to bathe in deep pits of earth. He died, mad, in 1794.

"Ascending douches" (upward showers) recommended by 19th-century doctors for male reproductive disorders.

A German priest-turned-doctor, Father Kneipp, recommended walking in water to "relieve the lungs, expel gas from the stomach and remove headaches". He also encouraged his patients to walk on wet grass, to water the stone paths outside their homes and to stroll bare-foot in fresh snow.

Many 19th-century doctors believed that wrapping patients tightly in wet sheets and leaving them to chill for 15 minutes would cure all kinds of dangerous diseases.

ELECTRIC BATH, c.1890. A mild electric current was passed through the water, producing a tingling feeling. Meant to be soothing, it could be extremely dangerous.

SEA-BATHING became very fashionable in the early 19th century. Wealthy people flocked to the newly-built seaside towns. They entered the sea from "bathing machines" - tiny caravans.

Medicinal foot-baths at the mineral-rich natural springs, Arrowhead, California, 1926.

Bath inside a moving cable-car, c.1960, at Arita Springs, Japan. Bathers can enjoy beautiful mountain scenery while they relax.

Steam bath, 1940, used to treat exhausted soldiers returning from front line duty during World War II.

19TH CENTURY: DEATH OR DRAINS?

New, improved sewers, lavatories and drinking water supplies.

WHILE RICH INVALIDS were visiting spas, and rich connoisseurs were ordering exquisite chamber-pot stands, ordinary people in town and country were still getting water and disposing of waste in old–fashioned ways. On farms and in villages, where there was plenty of fresh earth and a good chance of fairly clean water, standards of health and hygiene were not too bad. Around 1800, country people were more likely to die from cold or hunger than from water-borne disease. But in crowded towns, conditions were bad.

In the 1830s, cholera, a deadly disease spread by sewage-polluted water, arrived in Europe from Asia. Millions of people died. Typhoid fever, another disease caused by bad hygiene, was rife. Governments realized that urgent action was necessary. Until well-planned sewage systems, including drains, urinals and fresh drinking-water pumps, were installed in every major town, no one would be safe. At the same time, pioneering manufacturers, like Thomas Crapper and John Doulton, worked on new, improved domestic drainage installations and flush lavatory designs.

Rubber-sealed bucket for lavatory waste, collected once a week from city backyards.

Goux's Pail for lavatory waste had a thick absorbent lining. It could be sent back to the factory for emptying.

Reverend Moule's Closet automatically covered waste with earth or ashes when the sitter rose.

earth or ashes

Duckett's Slop Water Closet: (1) maid tips slops (dirty water) into sink; (2) slops run down into drain.

1

2

19th-century lavatory bowls, made of glazed stoneware and elaborately decorated.

Underground view of Duckett's Closet: (3) slops reach bucket; (4) bucket tips over, flushing waste into sewer (5).

WORKING PEOPLE in 19th-century cities lived crowded together in unhealthy slums, without drains or clean water. Millions died from diseases caused by drinking water polluted with sewage.

Digging deep trenches to carry the first ever sewers in Fleet Street, London 1845.

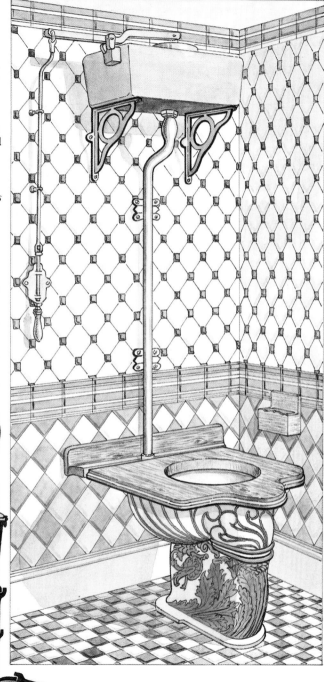

To try to prevent outbreaks of disease city councils employed street disinfectors, like these men, 1875.

Design for a men's urinal, 1881. It is decorated with tiles and ironwork. (Bottom) Same urinal ground-plan.

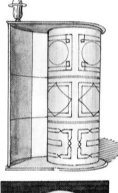

"The Lambeth" patent lavatory and overhead cistern (with chain to flush). Made by world-famous manufacturers, Doulton, c.1890.

3

4

5

19TH CENTURY: THE BEGINNINGS OF BATHROOMS

Baths now begin to have rooms of their own.

TUB FOR a sponge bath. The bather stood naked in the centre of the tub, and washed all over with a sponge.

(Right) 19TH-CENTURY shower. Cold water was pumped by hand into the overhead tank, then released by pulling a chain.

shower packed away for storage

Portable mahogany washstand "for the gentleman's room or library", c.1840. The lid could be closed for travel.

chamber-pot

Metal hip-bath, for bedroom use. It was filled with warm water carried upstairs by servants.

Sabot ("slipper") bath popular in Europe. Users sat upright, with only their heads visible.

AROUND 1800 B.C., there had been bathrooms – special rooms with facilities for washing and bathing – in King Minos's palace on the island of Crete. Yet bathrooms were not installed in many European royal palaces until the 19th century A.D. Before that, royals and nobles washed in tubs placed in their bedrooms, filled with water heated in a distant kitchen, and tidied away after use. The only alternative was a visit to a bathhouse or a spa.

Separate bathrooms cost a lot of money, and took up valuable space. That might explain why they were never found in ordinary people's homes. But most kings and nobles were rich. However, until the 19th century, not even their money could provide the three things an efficient bathroom needed: piped running water, good drainage (to cope with a whole bathful of water at once) and an instant, on-the-spot, source of heat.

Between 1850-1900, inventors and sanitary engineers devised ways of meeting all these requirements, and bathrooms began to be built – or converted from bedrooms – in all prosperous homes. Poor families could still not afford them, but they were able to buy cheap mass-produced tin baths and "coppers" for heating water, and to attend newly-built municipal baths.

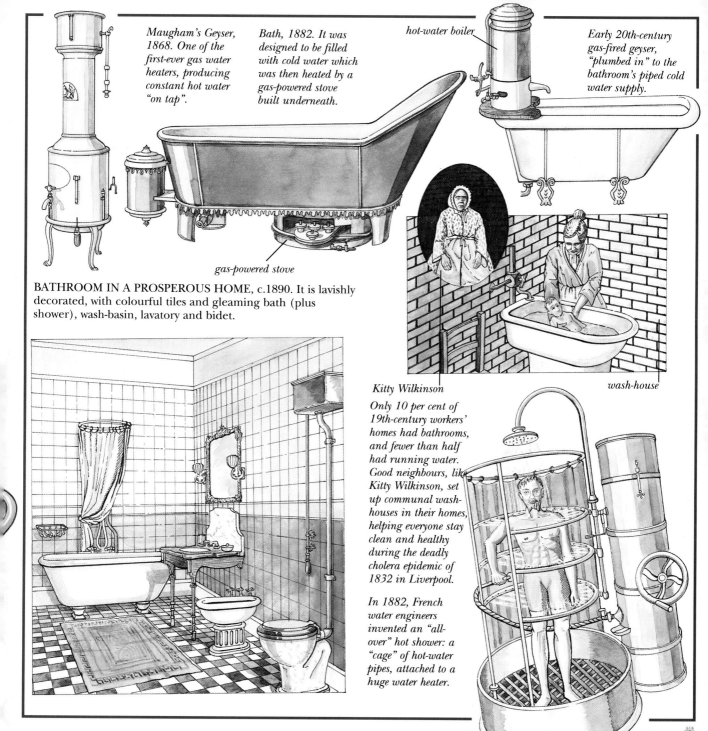

Maugham's Geyser, 1868. One of the first-ever gas water heaters, producing constant hot water "on tap".

Bath, 1882. It was designed to be filled with cold water which was then heated by a gas-powered stove built underneath.

hot-water boiler

Early 20th-century gas-fired geyser, "plumbed in" to the bathroom's piped cold water supply.

gas-powered stove

BATHROOM IN A PROSPEROUS HOME, c.1890. It is lavishly decorated, with colourful tiles and gleaming bath (plus shower), wash-basin, lavatory and bidet.

Kitty Wilkinson

wash-house

Only 10 per cent of 19th-century workers' homes had bathrooms, and fewer than half had running water. Good neighbours, like Kitty Wilkinson, set up communal wash-houses in their homes, helping everyone stay clean and healthy during the deadly cholera epidemic of 1832 in Liverpool.

In 1882, French water engineers invented an "all-over" hot shower: a "cage" of hot-water pipes, attached to a huge water heater.

ESSENTIALS AND EXTRAS

Aids to keeping clean down the centuries and around the world.

Romans used sponges (disinfected in salty water) or perfumed wool as wipes.

WATER BY ITSELF is sometimes not enough for hygiene. In past civilizations, people have used many different substances to clean themselves. They have also relied on herbs and flowers to act as disinfectants or air fresheners. Factory-made toilet paper was a 19th-century invention. It was first manufactured in the 1860s, by James Alcock, a British industrialist. His new product sold only slowly at first. Some people were too embarassed to ask for it in shops. However, the idea of toilet paper was not new. Wealthy Chinese people had used hand-made paper for centuries. In the Middle Ages, 15,000 sheets (about 8 cm square) of thick, soft, perfumed paper were supplied to the Chinese emperor's family every year. From the 18th century on, Europeans used bits of old newspaper.

Soap had been imported to ancient Rome from conquered Celtic and German lands. It was made of sheep's fat and wood ash, and was very harsh on the skin. Until the 19th century, many people preferred to use plain water or lye (ashes and water mixed) for washing, or, if they could afford it, lotions made from honey, almond oil and flowering plants. New, gentle soaps were invented by 19th-century chemists.

moss

Native American women used dried moss to make disposable nappies for babies.

Viking lavatories were deep pits, surrounded by wicker fencing. They used rags, animal bones or oyster shells as wipes.

oyster shells

pottery shards

moss

Wipes throughout the centuries have included:
1 Twigs and dried grass
2 Old feathers
3 Newspapers
4 Hard paper
5 Soft tissue
6 Moist wipes

Pears soap (left) was developed by Andrew Pears (born 1789), a Cornish chemist. The company he founded was one of the first to advertise their products widely, using "glamour" pictures (below).

Elderflower

In the 19th century, soap began to be mass-produced. A whole new factory town, Port Sunlight, was built in northern England, named after the soap made there.

For centuries, housewives and apothecaries made cleansers and cosmetics from beeswax, lanolin and plants. Twigs were chewed as natural tooth brushes.

Wild rose

Saponaria

twig toothbrush

cutting lavender

Flowers and herbs were added to baths simply to make washing more pleasant. This medieval manuscript shows that, for some lords, bathing could be a very luxurious experience.

Lavender

Deeply-ingrained dirt and patches of hard skin could be rubbed away with a pumice stone – solidified lava thrown up by an erupting volcano.

19TH CENTURY: WEIRD AND WONDERFUL

Bathtime technology reaches new extremes.

IN 1851, British manufacturers staged a massive exhibition of new technology at the Crystal Palace in London. It was designed to show off thousands of weird and wonderful inventions, and to proclaim Britain's place as "the workshop of the world". In the years that followed, other major industrial nations – France, Germany, Belgium and the USA – all held similar displays of their latest machinery. There was very little, it seemed, that could not be mass-produced to make life "better".

This international fascination with technology gave rise to many devices designed for keeping clean. Some were novelties, others were constructed for serious use. Many were concerned to halt the spread of illnesses that 19th-century people found embarrassing – urinary infections or sexually-transmitted disease. People believed these could be caught from dirty lavatory seats.

In spite of their modernity, most of these bath-time inventions relied on handymen, housemaids and cleaners to assemble them or to clear up after they had been used. They were produced by labourers working long hours in terrible conditions, in ironworks, quarries and mines. "Progress" did not always benefit everyone.

Turkish bath 1873. It was heated by a wood-burning stove, and fitted with castors, for easy movement.

cistern

foot pedals

French shower, 1878. The bather controlled the flow of water by "walking" on foot pedals.

English multi-purpose bath, 1904, with heat, light, water, steam, and an enclosing "lid", for taking a Turkish bath.

metal cover

heating apparatus

light bulbs

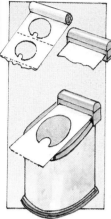

German exercise bath with rowing machine, 1901. The bather sat on a wheeled trolley in the bath, and created waves by pulling on the oars.

Disposable paper cover for lavatory seats, invented by Foettinger, an Austrian inn-keeper in 1902.

French Velo-Douche (bike-shower), 1897. It was inspired by the popular craze for cycling. As the bather pedalled, water from the shower basin was pumped up to the spray head.

German ladies' urinal, 1903. It fitted under long full skirts that made other lavatories difficult to use.

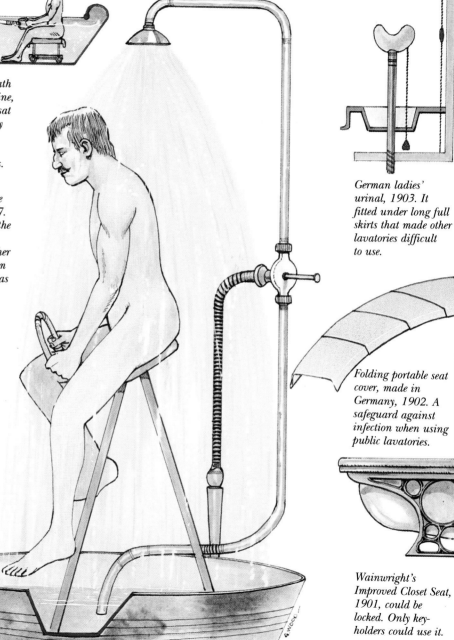

Folding portable seat cover, made in Germany, 1902. A safeguard against infection when using public lavatories.

The Velo-Douche (right) was created for exercise, and washing. Water was constantly recycled.

Wainwright's Improved Closet Seat, 1901, could be locked. Only key-holders could use it.

20th Century: Clean Water for All?

Water and sewage systems in rich and poor lands.

1 Oblong, 1920s

"Even the smallest house must have its fitted bath", wrote *Ideal Home* magazine in 1922. This was good, hygienic advice. But the homes of many poor people did not have fully functional bathrooms before the 1950s, and millions of people living in underdeveloped countries still do not have clean water, baths or proper sewage systems. Charities and politicians have called this a scandal. But it seems likely that in the year 2000 around a third of the world's population will not have basic modern facilities for keeping clean. Diseases carried by polluted water, such as polio and diptheria, have been almost eliminated in wealthy countries thanks to mass immunization and public health campaigns. But they still kill thousands of children every day in other parts of the world.

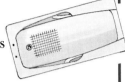

2 Water-saving, non-slip panel, 1980s

In contrast, bathrooms in the richer nations get bigger and more luxurious. Like the ancient Greeks and Romans, people aim to combine keeping fit with keeping clean. They take baths for pleasure and relaxation. Hotels and resorts join in, offering "thalassotherapy" (seaweed baths).

3 Deep oval, with handles, 1970s

Elaborate bathrooms – and well-trained personal servants – could be found in rich houses in many parts of the world.

Working-class families were lucky to be able to afford a bath from a tin bucket, in a chilly scullery.

Bidets were first used in France in the 18th century. They were designed to match lavatories.

4 Corner bath, 1980s

Bath with seat for use by people with disabilities, 1970s.

BATHROOM COMBINED with fitness centre, for total body care. American, 1980s.

THE SAUNA has underfloor heating. Water sprinkled on the hot rocks creates steam.

NEW VILLAGE WELL, providing water for drinking and washing, Cambodia, 1993. Simple projects like this can transform peoples' lives.

MODERN SCANDINAVIAN sauna, based on traditional Viking steam bath designs.

PAST AND FUTURE: MANAGING WASTE

New solutions to an age-old problem — and what about space?

MODERN WAYS of keeping clean solve public health problems. But people are beginning to realize that they can cause problems of their own. The environment can be seriously damaged by careless waste disposal, or by thoughtless use of chemicals designed to wash clothes and disinfect homes. Many beaches are horribly polluted by sewage, and wildlife in rivers and streams has been killed. (We cannot always rely on rainfall to provide enough water; but dams and reservoirs have been criticized for the environmental devastation they cause.)

Supplying pure water costs money and uses energy; environmentalists advise that we should no longer take deep baths but have showers, which use less water, instead. In recent years, traditional waste-disposal techniques, such as earth closets, have been re-evaluated and found to be surprisingly effective.

Space lavatory. The user stops him/herself floating away by holding handles.

In future centuries, waste management looks likely to be a major problem on earth. Scientists are already studying techniques developed for use in space, where water supplies and sewage disposal facilities are both limited.

Lavatory based on traditional designs in an ecological house, Wales, 1980s. After a year in the decomposition pit, the sewage turns into compost for garden use.

Compost waste-disposal system, Wales, 1980s. Lavatory waste, kitchen scraps and waste paper all rot in the underground pit to create safe organic fertilizer.

Electrically-powered "BioLet®" lavatory, for use in ecologically sensitive sites such as Antarctica. It uses heat to dry waste, leaving only a small volume of safe, dry powder.

Lavatories, called "waste-management compartments", are fitted to most spacecraft. This was used in Skylab:

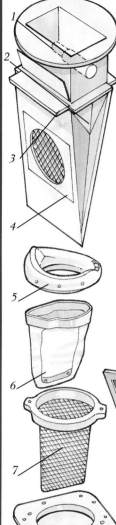

1 Strip-off cover, to stop contents floating round craft in zero gravity

2 Finger-thimble, to help wipe waste away

3 Lid with strong seal

4 Collector bag with water vapour escape vent

Inside the collector bag:

5 Hinged seat fits on top and folds away

6 Bag to collect waste

7 Mesh outer bag to stop waste escaping

8 Strong outer cover, with gas outlet (fitted with filter)

Astronauts (male and female) used funnels attached to waste-pipes for urination. The urine was dumped in space, where it froze to form a ring of crystals round the spaceship.

Space shower, used on board Skylab. Users were sprayed with water and liquid soap. The outer casing stopped droplets flying everywhere.

When working outside spacecraft, astronauts wore "faecal containment systems" (very absorbent underpants) inside their suits.

CONVENIENT

and clean.

The Great Bath at Mohenjo-Daro measures almost 10 metres x 7 metres, and is 2.5 metres deep. Archaeologists think it may have been used by temple worshippers – or else as a reservoir for sacred crocodiles.

Nine great aqueducts carried water to the city of Rome; together, they were 425 kilometres long. They carried over 350 million litres of water every 24 hours.

The Romans distrusted soap; they thought it was bad for the skin and that it would bleach and weaken their glossy black hair.

Roman grafitti: 'To hunt, to bathe, to play: that's what makes life worth living.'

By the 3rd century B.C., the Japanese were famous for their cleanliness. As well as bathing in hot springs and warm volcanic mud, they also worshipped the wild animals they met at these holy 'cleaning places'.

The Prophet Muhammad (died 632), leader of the first Muslim community at Medina in Arabia, was reported to have said 'Cleanliness is half the faith'. Western travellers to Muslim lands admired Muslim cleanliness and their public baths.

The Viking name for Saturday means 'bath-day'.

A medieval joke claimed that peasants only washed twice during their lives: when they were baptised and before they were buried. But King John of England (1167-1216) was different: he boasted that he took a bath every three weeks.

In 1335, there was enough liquid waste in the ditch of London's Newgate Prison – which was 3 metres wide – to float a boat.

The medieval French philosopher Peter Abelard (1079-1142) wrote a book of instructions for nuns.

He advised them to change their clothes once a week.

Some baths were very comfortable. In 1403 Princess Margaret of Flanders (Belgium) purchased 40 metres of canvas to line two bathtubs, and some fancy red cloth for their canopies.

Toothbrushes were invented in China. They were introduced to Europe around 1650.

In 1679, a group of Turkish merchants built London's first public baths since Roman times, modelled on Middle Eastern steam baths.

In the 1840s, few households in Paris, the capital city of France, had bathrooms – or baths. Thanks to big ironworks nearby a new, thriving business grew up: you could hire a metal bath for the night, to take home with you.

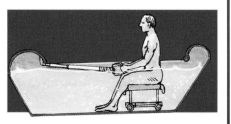

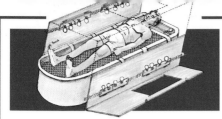

The first paying public conveniences were opened in London in 1851, at the Great Exhibition at Crystal Palace. Over 827,280 visitors to the exhibition used them, resulting in a profit of £1,790.

Soon, many other 'halting stations' were built. Entry cost a penny – giving rise to the popular saying: 'spending a penny' for 'going to the lavatory'. Some of these new lavatories were so splendid that they became known as 'temples of convenience'.

In the 19th century, Dr Nichols' 'Sanitary Soap' was advertised as 'Deodorising, Antiseptic, Disinfectant . . . an Admirable Dentifrice (toothpaste) and makes a Perfect Shaving Soap. Can be used by Ladies for the face without fear and gives a singular softness to the hands . . .'

In 1906, the Ritz hotel in Paris installed a bath in every bedroom – the first hotel to do so. Other top hotels soon copied the Ritz.

In 1911, in Britain, the Coal Miners Act made it compulsory for mine-owners to provide pit-head baths at mines where two-thirds of the miners said they wanted them, and to pay for half the cost of running them. The miners paid the other half.

In 1914, the German ocean liner *Imperator* became the first great ship to be built with a swimming pool on board. It was modelled on Ancient Roman baths, and ornamented with Ancient Egyptian designs.

In the 1920s, the city of Aurora, Illinois, USA, passed a law saying that all citizens must take a bath at least once a week, or go to prison.

Also in the 1920s, an American organization called the 'Cleanliness Institute' ran a 'Cleanliness Crusade', with this slogan:
'Clean hands and hearts may hope
To find the way to happiness
By using lots of soap.'

British colonial administrators, working in distant parts of the Empire, invented all kinds of unusual lavatories in harsh, hostile lands, where there was no running water. The 'smoking pit latrine' (1930s) consisted of six wooden seats fixed across a deep trench filled with smoke from a constantly-burning fire. The smoke kept flies away, and the heat killed germs.

In 1929, Robert Stallworth, an American inventor, designed a rubber and asbestos chamber-pot, warmed by electricity. It was meant for winter use.

In 1966, a hairdresser in Chicago, USA, invented a motorised lavatory. The seat was divided into two halves, which vibrated rapidly, gently, or at two different speeds, massaging the user.

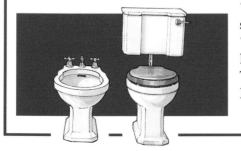

GLOSSARY

Ammonia Strong-smelling chemical compound, which can be extracted from stale urine. It has the power to dissolve grease.

Apodyterium Roman word for changing room.

Apothecaries People who studied chemistry and sold simple medicines.

Aqueduct Channel (often built high above the ground) for carrying water over long distances.

Bathing machine A tiny caravan, which could be wheeled into the sea so that people, especially women, bathe from it in privacy.

Bedpan Bowl used by invalids as a portable lavatory.

Bidet Low basin you can sit on.

Bronze Metal alloy: tin and copper mixed.

Caldarium Hottest room in a Roman baths.

Cesspit Deep pit where sewage is stored.

Cistern Tank for storing fresh water.

Close stool Chair or stool with a built-in pot, used as a lavatory.

Copper Large metal tins often made of copper – heated by gas jets underneath.

Dub To touch someone lightly on the shoulders with a sword: part of the ceremony of becoming a knight.

Earth closet Lavatory without water; waste is covered by a sprinkling of earth.

Earthenware Cheap, coarse pottery, often with a white or brownish glaze.

Ewer Jug for carrying water.

Frigidium Coldest room in a Roman baths.

Garderobe French word for wardrobe, used by rich medieval people to mean lavatory. Garderobes were often just a bucket in a cupboard, or a seat over a hole in the wall.

Glazed Covered with glaze – a thin, glassy layer on top of pottery.

Goblet Wide-mouthed cup on a stem. Used for drinking wine.

Hogan Hut made of earth-covered branches.

Insula (plural insulae) Roman word for a block of flats.

Jacuzzi Bath with waves and bubbles, produced by high-pressure water jets along the sides.

Lanolin Grease from sheeps' wool.

Laver Small, built-in wash-basin.

Laxatives Medicines to cure constipation.

Lay-brothers Men who lived in

monasteries and helped monks.

Lye Mixture of wood-ash and soap, used for washing.

Mahogany Fine, reddish-brown wood from tropical rainforest trees.

Ottoman The period of Middle Eastern history when the Ottoman dynasty (from Turkey) ruled. Roughly, the 16th to 19th centuries.

Pages Young boys who waited at tables and ran errands.

Pharisees Jewish religious experts.

Plunge bath Bath deep enough to stand up in.

Pomander Ball of sweet-smelling medicinal herbs and spices.

Pumice Stone thrown up during volcanic eruptions. Used to scrape away flakes of dead skin.

Quack Fake doctor.

Ritual Ceremony, often with a religious purpose.

Sadducees Jewish religious experts.

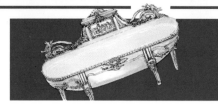

Salon Word used in 'polite' society for a sitting room.

Samurai Japanese warrior.

Sauna Viking steam bath, made by pouring water over stones heated red-hot in a fire. Followed by a plunge into a lake or into the snow.

Scullery Small back room, used for washing clothes and dishes. Often without running water.

Shaman Holy man or woman, who claimed to be able to communicate with spirits.

Sitz bath Bath where the sitting bather was sprayed with hot and cold water. Meant to improve the circulation of the blood.

Slipper bath Covered bath,

shaped like an enormous shoe.

Sludge Sewage solids, like sticky, slimy mud.

Squires Young men who helped knights get ready for battle and who looked after their weapons and armour.

Stink trap Layer of water (trapped in pipes) that stopped unpleasant lavatory and drain smells rising into rooms.

Strigil Metal scraper, used to remove sweat and dirt.

Sudatorium Roman word for 'sweat room'; part of a Roman baths.

Tepidarium Roman word for 'warm room'; part of a Roman baths.

Terracotta Red-coloured, unglazed clay.

Tonsure Special hairstyle worn by monks.

Vapour bath Bath where the bather sits in a cloud of steam.

Wudu Ritual washing before Muslim prayers.

INDEX

Artists David Antram pages 8, 9, 14-15, 36-37, 40-41, 42-43; Simon Calder pages 12-13; John James pages 26-27, Joe McEwan pages 10-11, 16, 17, 18-19, 20-21, 24-25, Lee Peters pages 32-33, 34–35; Carolyn Scrace pages 22-23; Gerald Wood pages 28-29, 30-31, 38-39.